The House of Fun

Iris Howden

Published in association with
The Basic Skills Agency

Hodder Murray
A MEMBER OF THE HODDER HEADLINE GROUP

00027317
062803
428.6 HOW
BAT
STANDARD LOAN
Tr ⟹ 6th fom

Orders: please contact Bookpoint Ltd, 130 Milton Park, Abingdon, Oxon OX14 4SB.
Telephone: (44) 01235 827720. Fax: (44) 01235 400454. Lines are open 9.00–6.00,
Monday to Saturday, with a 24-hour message answering service. Visit our website at
www.hoddereducation.co.uk

First published in 2005 by
Hodder Murray, a member of the Hodder Headline Group
338 Euston Road
London NW1 3BH

Impression number   10 9 8 7 6 5 4 3 2 1
Year   2010 2009 2008 2007 2006 2005

Cover illustration by Janos Jantner/Beehive Illustration
Illustrations by Pulsar Studio/Beehive Illustration
Typeset by Transet Limited, Coventry, England.
Printed in Great Britain by Athenaeum Press Ltd, Gateshead, Tyne & Wear.

A catalogue record for this title is available from the British Library

ISBN-10 0 340 90055 5
ISBN-13 9 780340 900550

Contents

1

In the Arcade

'Turn that thing off,' Scott's mum said.
'I want to hoover the carpet.
Go out and get some fresh air.
You spend all day playing games.
You're becoming an addict.'
'No way!' Scott said, but he got up.
He switched off his Play Station.

It was the school holidays. Scott was bored.
He called for his mate, Terry.
Scott told Terry what his mum had said.
'She called me an addict,' he said.
'Well, you do play games a lot,' Terry said.
'On the Play Station, on the computer
and on your Game Boy.'
'So, I like playing games,' Scott said.
'But I'm not an addict.'

They walked to the town centre.
'Let's go in the arcade,' Scott said.
'Play on the machines.'
'I've got no money,' Terry said.
'We could just watch,' Scott said.

He loved being in the arcade.
Seeing the machines light up.
Hearing the noises they made.
It was exciting.

They hung around for a time.
Terry soon got bored. He went home.
Scott was fed up watching.
He wanted to play a game.
To get his hands on the controls.

Then he saw something on the floor.
It was a ten-pound note.
Someone must have lost it.
Scott knew he should hand it in,
but he was dying to play a game.
He went to the office for change.

Scott chose a game called Race Track.
He always got a high score on that.
He knew how to avoid a crash.
How to take the bends.
When to slow down and speed up.
He wanted to beat his own lap time.

He played six games in a row.
A woman in a red jacket watched him play.
'You're very good,' she said.
'You must play a lot.'
She held out a card.
Her nails were the same red as her jacket.

Scott read the words on the card.
'Demon Games Ltd', it said.
'My name's Lara,' the woman told him.
'I'm a rep for a games firm.
We're looking for young people
to try out our games.
Would you be interested?'
Scott nodded.
First the tenner and now this.
It must be his lucky day.

4

Lara gave him a letter to take home.
'Ask your parents to sign this,' she said.
'To say you can take part.'
The letter said he would be away
for a week, trying out new games.

There was no way Scott's mum
would let him do that.
But he really wanted to go.
He would have to forge his mum's signature.
He had done it before,
to get out of PE at school.
He took the letter to his bedroom.
'Jean Wilson', he wrote.
He took care not to rush it.
His mum's signature was very neat.

Then he went downstairs.
'Terry wants me to go camping,' he said.
'For a week. At his uncle's farm.
Is that OK?'
'Yes,' his mum said. 'It will do you good.
Stop you from playing those silly games.'

2
House Mates

Lara drove Scott to a big house
out in the country.
She led him into a room.
Five other kids were sitting there.
'This is the House of Fun,' she said.
'You are here to enjoy yourselves.'

Scott looked at the others.
There were two boys, Vince and Paul.
Two older kids, Anna and Jason.
There was one other girl.
She was small and pretty.
Her name was Zoe.

'Now for the house rules,' Lara said.
'Hand over your mobile phones.
You can't go out or speak to anyone else.
The new games must be kept secret.
The Game Master will tell you what to do.
Cameras in every room will watch you play.
Have fun.'
She left the room.

'This is like *Big Brother*,' Anna said.

The six of them talked about the games
they liked best.
Lunch was laid out ready for them.
There was lots of nice food on the table.
Cold drinks in the fridge.
Staff dressed in black waited on them.
'It's better than *Big Brother*,' Anna said.
'We don't have to cook or wash up!'

In bed that night, Scott thought
it had been a great day.
His housemates were good fun.
He had his own room and bathroom.
And he would get paid for playing games.
Lara had said he would get £1000.

Scott wanted to look outside.
He pulled back the curtain.
There were bars on the window.
He went to the door. It was locked.
His smart room was like a prison cell.

3
Playing Games

The next day they met the Game Master.
He was a tall thin man.
He had a bald head and cold blue eyes.
He did not say much and he never smiled.
Scott thought he was creepy.

They were put into pairs.
Vince was with Paul, Anna with Jason.
Scott and Zoe were together.
They went to different rooms.
'The computers are set up,' the Game Master said.
'Games are over there.'
'He's weird,' Zoe whispered as he left.

'Never mind him,' Scott said.
'Look at these games!
Which do you want?'

'I like the look of Spider Trap,' Zoe said.
'OK. I'll try Gang War,' Scott said.

At the end of the day, the six got together.
'What a day!' Vince said.

'Those Play Stations are wicked.'
'We had arcade machines,' Anna said.
'Cool,' Scott said. 'I hope we get to try them all.'

For two days they tested games.
At teatime they talked about them.
On the third day, Vince was very quiet.
He looked upset and went to bed early.
His room was next to Scott's.

In the middle of the night, Scott woke up.
He heard noises coming from next door.
Then he heard the Game Master's deep voice.
'Get him out of here,' he said.

At breakfast Vince was missing.
'Where's Vince?' Paul asked.

12

'He's gone home,' the Game Master said.
'He had a stomach bug.'

The next day Anna looked ill.
She hardly spoke.
She didn't eat any tea.
'What's wrong?' Zoe asked.
'I want to go home,' Anna said.

Then she looked up at the camera on the wall.
She wrote a note and passed it round.
'This place is evil', it said.
Next morning, she had gone as well.

There were only two days left.

'I'm ready to go home now,' Jason said.
'How about you?'
'Not me,' Scott said.
'I could play games for ever.'

4
The Vampire

It was day six.
Scott switched on the Play Station.
A picture came on the screen.
'Night of the Vampire', it said.
'How about this?' Scott asked.
'It looks scary,' Zoe said.
'I hate vampires, but I'll play if you want.'

The screen said, 'Enter your name'.
Zoe put her name in. Scott put 'SW'.
They played for a while.
The game was quite hard.
They had to collect weapons
to get to the next level.

Zoe got a sword.
'That's no good,' Scott said.
'You need a stake to kill a vampire.'

Scott got to level two.
Then he made it to level three.
'Yes,' he shouted. 'I've won!'
'I've got the stake.
I'm in the castle of the vampire.'

Suddenly the room went dark.
The walls looked different.
They were not white any more.
They were made of grey stone.
Zoe looked scared.
'What's happening?' she asked.

The door opened.
A tall man dressed in black came in.
Scott thought it was the Game Master,
but it was not.
The man had a white face.
He had pointed fangs with blood on them.

It was a vampire.

The vampire went towards Zoe.
She began to scream.
'Help me, Scott,' she shouted.

Scott was scared, but he ran at the vampire.
He waved the stake at him.
The vampire pushed Scott through a doorway.
It was very dark inside.
Suddenly Scott was falling, falling, falling.

5

A Nightmare Day

Scott woke up in bed.
He had a bad headache.
He got dressed and went downstairs.
Zoe was at the table eating breakfast.
'You're late,' she said.
She looked quite normal.
As if nothing had happened.

Scott looked at her neck.
If the vampire had bitten her,
fang marks would show.
There was not a mark on Zoe's neck.
'About the vampire game ...,' Scott said.
'What about it?' Zoe said. 'You won.
Big deal. I'll win next time.'

Zoe looked happy.
She didn't remember seeing the vampire!
Scott knew he had not dreamed it.
The vampire had been for real.
He knew that Vince and Anna
must have seen things too.
Bad things that had made them want to go home.
If they had gone home!

Suddenly Scott felt very afraid.
He went into the hall. Maybe he could sneak out.
Two of the staff stood by the front door.
'Where are you going?' one asked him.
'It's time to start the games.'

The Game Master came up.
He grabbed Scott by the arm.
He pulled him into the room
with arcade machines. Zoe was waiting.
'Wow,' she said. 'War Zone looks good.
Come and play, Scott.'
Scott felt jumpy.
He didn't want to play.
He had a bad feeling about the games.

Zoe handed him the controls. It was like a gun.
They had to shoot at armed men.
The machine made loud noises.
Like guns firing, bullets flying past.

'You have to duck,' Zoe told him.
'Or you lose a life.'

Scott was scared that the game
would become real.
If a bullet hit him, he might die.
Soon Zoe was way ahead.
'What's the matter, Scott?' she asked.
'You're half asleep. I've won again.'
It said 'Game over' on the screen.

They played lots of different games.
Scott could not relax.
He began to sweat when they played
Deep Sea Dive.
If it became real they might drown.
He felt sick when they played
Lost in Space.
If that became real, he might never get home.

The last game was called Jungle Quest.
In the game, Scott and Zoe had to find
a chest full of gold.
'Choose your character,' Zoe said.

They played for a while.
Scott sent his character into a cave.
There was a chest at the back.
'Open it', it said on the screen.

Scott opened it.
There was no gold inside.
The chest was full of snakes.
Scott tried to shut it again.
It would not close.
Snakes began to crawl out of it.

Scott hated snakes.
He was really afraid of them.
He couldn't even look at them on the screen.
He hated their scaly skin.
Their beady little eyes.
The way their tongues flicked in and out.

'What's the matter?' Zoe asked.
Scott couldn't answer.
He felt something crawl on to his hand.
Snakes were coming out of the machine.
Lots of snakes. All different sizes.

Scott began to panic.
He ran about, waving his arms.
Trying to shake the snakes off.
He looked down.
There were snakes all over the floor.

He screamed as the snakes
began to crawl up his legs
and around his body.
They wound around his neck.
Scott couldn't breathe.
'Help me, Zoe,' he gasped.
Then he blacked out.

6

Home Again

Scott woke up in bed.
He knew he had not been dreaming.
Those snakes had been for real.
If he shut his eyes, he could still see them.
Feel them crawling over his skin.
He got dressed and went downstairs.

All the other kids had left.
'Pack your bag,' the Game Master said.
'Lara will drive you home.'

Scott was so glad to hear this,
he ran upstairs.
He couldn't wait
to get out of this horrible place.

Back home, he ran into the house.
His mum was in the kitchen.
He gave her a hug.
'What's up, Scott?' she said.
'Why are you back so soon?'

'What do you mean?' Scott was puzzled.
He had been away for a week.

'Well, you went yesterday,' his mum said.
'You only stayed one day.
What happened?'
Scott made up an excuse.
He said Terry's uncle had been ill.

There was a newspaper on the table.
He read the date: Sunday 5th August.
That was very odd.
Lara had picked him up on Saturday, the 4th.

He went round to see Terry.
He tried to tell him what had happened.
Terry didn't believe him.
'Come off it, Scott,' he said.

They walked to the town centre.
'Let's go in the café,' Terry said.
'I'll buy you a coffee. Clear your head.'

Two girls were sitting at a table.
One of them was Zoe.
Scott went over to her.
She would know he was telling the truth.

'Zoe,' he said. 'Am I glad to see you!'
Zoe looked at him.
'Who are you?' she said.
'I've never seen you before in my life.'

'But Zoe,' Scott said,
'you must remember me.
The House of Fun. The games we played.'
Zoe spoke to Terry.
'Tell your mate to get lost,' she said.
'I don't know what he's talking about.'

Scott walked home feeling upset.
Nothing was normal any more.
Maybe he was going mad.

The only thing that cheered him up
was the thought of the money.
Lara had said he would get a cheque
for £1000 in the post.

Scott was up early, waiting for the postman.
He heard a letter drop through the box.
He ran into the hall.
He tore the envelope open.
Yes, there it was. A cheque for £1000.
It was made out to him, Scott Wilson.
The writing was in black ink.

He held it up to the light
with a big grin on his face.
Suddenly the writing began to fade.
First the date faded away.
Then the amount, £1000.
Last of all his name, Scott Wilson,
disappeared from the cheque.

All that was left
was the face of the Game Master
smiling back at him.